3/03

D0643030

A Protocol for Touch

Previous winners of the Vassar Miller Prize in Poetry
Scott Cairns, Series Editor

1993   *Partial Eclipse* by Tony Sanders
       selected by Richard Howard

1994   *Delirium* by Barbara Hamby
       selected by Cynthia Macdonald

1995   *The Sublime* by Jonathan Holden
       selected by Yusef Komunyakaa

1996   *American Crawl* by Paul Allen
       selected by Sydney Lea

1997   *Soul Data* by Mark Svenvold
       selected by Heather McHugh

1998   *MOVING & ST RAGE* by Kathy Fagan
       selected by T. R. Hummer

A Protocol for Touch

Constance Merritt

Winner, Vassar Miller Prize in Poetry
Eleanor Wilner, Judge

University of North Texas Press
Denton, Texas

Copyright © 1999 Constance Merritt

First edition 2000

All rights reserved.
Printed in the United States of America.

5   4   3   2   1

Permissions:
University of North Texas Press
PO Box 311336
Denton TX 76203-1336
940-565-2142

The paper used in this book meets the minimum requirements of the American
National Standard for Permanence of Paper for Printed Library Materials,
z39.48.1984. Bind materials have been chosen for durability.

Library of Congress Cataloging-in-Publication Data

Merritt, Constance, 1966–
A protocol for touch : poems / by Constance Merritt.–1st ed.
p.   cm.
ISBN 1-57441-083-0 (pbk. : alk. paper)
I. Title.
PS3563.E74536   P76   2000
811'.54–dc21   99-054652

Design by Angela Schmitt
Cover art by Jonathon Green, *Bathing*, 1990, Oil on canvas 51" x 70"
Norton Museum of Art, West Palm Beach, Florida

811.52
MER
2000

Acknowledgments

Grateful acknowledgment is made to the editors of the following periodicals, in which some of the poems in this volume first appeared:

American Literary Review: "Genesis," "Ghazal," "Miserykids on the Line"
Callaloo: "Avant Garde," "Lullaby," "The Mute Swan"
The Disability Rag & Resource: "The Bride," "Etude for Memory and Guitar," "A Study in Perspective"
Higginson Journal: "The Mother's Seduction"
Nebraska Humanities: "The Check-Out Lady at the IGA," "Roses"
Phoebe: "Motion"
Ploughshares: "Woman of Color"
Prairie Schooner: "Black Iris," "Self-Portrait: Lilith, Eve," "Separation"
Quarterly West: "Etude for Memory and Guitar"
Rocky Mountain Review: "Bitches on the Bright Side," "A Protocol for Touch"
The Women's Review of Books: "Offering"

"Lullaby," "The Mute Swan," and "Woman of Color" also appear in *American Poetry: The Next Generation* (Pittsburgh: Carnegie Mellon UP, 2000).

for my mother, father, and grandmother—
first strands in the braid of life

Physical wholeness is not something we have barring accident; it is itself accidental, an accident of infancy, like a baby's fontanel or the egg-tooth on a hatchling.

—*Annie Dillard*

Contents

•

III.

IV.

Overtures

•

The Mute Swan

•

White silence on the water pulls me in and under. And I know it is a lady.

The impossibility of naming her desire has kept her white and beautiful, while she has kept our secrets. She holds them deep within the throat of her graceful neck, and it is hard to say whether, when she bows her head, she is praying to take voice or to go on giving silence.

It is also hard to say whether hers is the silence of before speaking or after. Almost as hard as saying nothing.

•

Woman of Color

•

The splendid coat that wrapped the favored son
In fevered dreams of adulation
And turned his brothers' hearts from jealousy
To rage (*Behold, this dreamer comes.*)—though long
Since rent and soaked in blood, dried and decomposed—
Arrives through the long centuries over
Sea and land, the unexpected birthright
Of this particular girl. Its separate
Magic beads and threads spill onto the floor
Indistinguishable from alphabet
Blocks, the many pieces of her country,
And its citizens loud and teeming from
Their cramped Crayola crayon box. Each state,
Each letter has a color, a shape, its own,
Soft curves and sharp angles, compassionate
Contours promising something not hers to keep,
An abundance utterly unasked for and
Nearly impossible to give. *What is*
This dream that thou hast dreamed? Shall I and thy
Mother and thy brethren indeed come
To bow down ourselves to thee to the earth?

It is loneliness that bows her head, that breaks
Her free from silence's sweet spell, spilling
Her voice onto the brittle air, breathless
In its rush: green of sea, pine, forest, spring;
Blue of midnight, cerulean, cornflower;
Sky, navy, cadet, and royal blue; blue

4

Violet, turquoise, aquamarine; teal blue,
Blue green, periwinkle; burnt and raw
Sienna, bittersweet, brick and in-
Dian red, goldenrod and thistle, white.
And exile enters here, the lull and pull
Of distance between the voice's deepest source
And its unmappable destinations.
And they sat down to eat bread and they lifted
Up their eyes and looked, and, behold, a company
Of Ishmaelites came from Gilead with
Their camels bearing spicery and balm
And myrrh going to carry it down to
Egypt. And Judah said, what profit is it
If we slay our brother and conceal his blood?
Let us sell him for he is our brother and our flesh.

For her there is no Egypt to seduce
With strange, mad song, no famished countrymen
Falling to their knees and near enough
To make her tremble afraid she will be tender
Instead of stern. Instead there is only
This brilliant coat, a gift of love, that leaves
Her vulnerable to cold and knowing eyes
Until it seems she has no skin at all
Except for silence, except the weave of words:
Hound's-tooth, gingham, tulle, eyelet, chambray;
Broad-cloth, denim, paisley, linen, wool.
Her dreams grow full of birdsong; each bird says
Its name: Cardinalis Cardinalis,
Anas Carolinensis, Cyanthus
Latirostris, Mimus Polyglottos,
Cyanocitta Stelleri, Agelaius
Phoenecius—over and over,
Until, finally, sure it's meant for her,
She gently stirs the waters' smooth bright skin,
And bursting from the deep into the world,
Its fear, its hurt, its roar; she tries her tongue.

I.

Oasis

Not alone, but invisible,
I am choked by smoke and loneliness
And long to leave this place.

I am afraid of flying
And a great distance from the sea.

Still I must not stay here
Swilling beer like bad water
And dreaming of the sea.

Outside the air is new,
And I breathe without trying—
The right way, from deep inside,
That makes the belly warm.
The sidewalk is cool beneath me,
And there is comfort in this wall
That marks outside from in.

An angel comes to me,
And we dance outside, inside
Each other's arms to music
Far away but close enough to feel.
We will never be close enough
Although we are too close
For dancing, comfort, breathing.
There is no salvation here. Just salt
And need that won't bear healing.

Beauty and the Beast

Before the mirror, scissors in hand,
You had thought to make yourself
Hideous, but it all came down to fashion.
And after only one week of shame,
You unveiled your shorn head
As one more prop in the masquerade.

There are only two masks you can wear,
And the choice is never yours
Except on those days when you choose
To stay in bed, refuse to be lured
To the closet, the mirror, to stand
As the verdict is read.

You believe that mirrors always lie,
And you believe the lies they tell
Because anything is preferable to bald truth,
To the gnawing knowledge that within you lies
Neither monstrousness nor beauty.

Struggling against your next breath
Or for it, you run between extremes,
Avoiding the real distance,
Which is no distance at all,
But an almost unbearable proximity
That puts everything within your reach
And keeps you far from touch,
Arriving just in time to watch
The show go on without your part.

•

Black Iris

•

after Georgia O'Keeffe

I.
So utterly open, indecently exposed
Or exquisitely closed upon themselves

I bring fresh-cut flowers wrapped in paper
In the park we talk of women

But it's not that simple
There are so many places between open and shut
And there's what we say without knowing

II.
Nobody sees a flower—really—we haven't time
I never remember to ask the color of her eyes

I am afraid *she* won't remember, won't be there
So I stop on the way and buy flowers

Shape, color, scent, and feel
There is no more than this
And she is pleased and embarrassed

III.
"Be modest in what you show me
I already see so much"

When she is very near I close my eyes

I do not know the names of birds or flowers
But always say someday I'll learn

IV.
In a few days she will throw these flowers out
With juice bottles and the daily news
They will not remain like this painted flower
Exacting more than is proper, more
Than admiration, which is inexpensive
And abundant in the world

I want them to see it whether they want to or not
I don't always know what I'm seeing or why

Sometimes I see a wound waiting for salt
Or healing, inviting cool interest
Or consuming love. And whether for comfort or shame
I want to clothe its nakedness in layers of soft petals

V.
I think of her neither as friend nor lover
And believe in truths as yet unsaid

She will say she feels unworthy of this poem
The way I feel in front of this painting
Or at her side

I want someone to know everything
The desire seems obscene

Like the dark interior of this painted flower
Pistils, stamens, anthers all in view

I never wanted to be this close to anything

Second Hand

It's the one that deftly picks the rhythm while the other frets, or flannel shirts and well-worn books culled from the DAV.

Or it's the frail neurotic, nervous from too much caffeine, who continually cleans the house of time, sweeping each second away.

Or the place where I ceased to chatter, forgot myself and you there watching me, and scarcely breathed as I caressed each finger and the little crotches in between.

Instead of Love

Absence registers itself in daily things:
The kettle quiet, the teacups so long clean,
The Scrabble kissed by dust upon the shelf,
And, afternoons, the paths that we once walked
With ease and regularity, stretched on
To destinations, indifferent to us.

We used to own those paths. I do not mean
Possessed, but owned as in to recognize
Or claim. Or rather they claimed us; we were
Possessed. We needed to be there, had to
Return in spite of snow and cold and our
Desire to touch another ground and call
It home. We longed for dangerous terrain,
Our fantasies all cliffs and oceans as
We made our way across the Jordan river
Along the paths and bridges made by men.

Instead of love we make believe. You lead
Me up from Hell into sweet air and sun,
Or I lead you, afraid I will look back
And loose the chains that hold the demons of
Your world at bay. The tenderness that we
Would lavish on ourselves if wholly free
Or young is spent upon this land
Of modest claims. And as for fevered dreams
We starve them in the cold, the price of Par-
Adise beyond our means. Though still we might,

In these last days, pretend we do not know
How each new shard of self reclaimed becomes
Just one more loss that we must suffer through.

•

Vandals

•

This house we could not enter, not even through
The back door or on the arm of our lover, night.
The landlord was no fool. He knew what might
Get started if he let us in. Knew
How sorely we decrease property value.
Look around you. Can you say he wasn't right?
See these handsome bruises. Drink in the blue
And laugh. Then show me the wounds I gave to you
Without a touch. Fuck love when we can fight
Like this. I tell you, baby, we be fierce!
[The conjugation's from *your* Tudor past.]

In juke joints, churches, and bad streets in town,
When a speaker moves in close, gets near brass tacks,
We say: Come on now, all right, break it down.

●

Roses

●

No word from you. I set my will to date
Men met by telephone who think my voice is
Sexy and won't believe I'm overweight
When I offer them a chance to cut their losses.
Each one must come to see the ugliness
I claim with his own eyes, suspecting lies
That gorgeous women tell. Unless it's sex
They all come running after, though no one tries
A thing. So with care I curl my hair, select
A dress, anxious to exchange one kind of danger
For another, and don't ask myself what I expect
To find. I'm eaten up by love, by anger
At you, at God. A nice man brings me flowers,
The price, a kiss. Left, I spit and brush for hours.

•

A Study in Perspective

•

I.
Looking at you was the hardest thing.

Taking off my clothes
While you stayed dressed,

II.
Nothing.

III.
My body a knife, my shoulder
Its blade, I cut a path before me.

Or sometimes I'm an apprentice ghost
Unsure in the art of haunting;

No one sees me as I pass.

IV.
No one sees me as I pass
Though someone is always looking,
Translating texts of skin and eyes
As: *our lives are whole without her.*

V.
The intention of the taker doesn't matter;
Shame lies only in not being had,
Pain in too much having.

VI.
If you weren't older by twenty years,
Superior in race, middle-class
By marriage, and *sighted*,
You couldn't whisper *strip*
And then refuse to do the same.

We get away with what we can,
And this poet gives what she gives.

VII.
Historically, it was a woman's fate, a slaves's:
Submission to a gaze s/he can't return.

VIII.
I am not you; that's you and not me.
From a distance the boundaries stay clear,
And fear lies coiled and sleeping in its place.

IX.
Up close, I look at you, give you
My body without its mask of blindness,
Allow you to see me, my eyes
As they work at seeing you.

And not because, as I have said,
I loved you more, or am most good,

Just well-rehearsed as vulnerable.

SIMMS LIBRARY
ALBUQUERQUE ACADEMY

•

Motion

•

Motion is the antithesis of faith.
Knowing this, your best recourse is to forget—
Turn your pillow, find that cooler space,
Shift from side to side to back to side.
Try sleeping on your stomach for awhile,
Limbs akimbo, then curled in a ball.

Rush past the childish giddiness at presence
Of one you love and get right down to sex,
And spare yourself a grace you can't sustain.
Make love in many cities. See only
Hotel rooms, adequate and clean. Eat in
Or dine in restaurant chains easily
Found most anywhere. Cities, like gods,
Demand escape or, at least, resistance.
A city will pursue you, and a life
Wasted in one small corner is destroyed
Everywhere.

I think of trees, of everything they bear,
How I have failed to know your naked body
Perfectly, the movements of your sleep, old scars,
Dull pain. How I've somehow failed to try
As hard as I might have some miles ago.

With every move desire grows less sharp,
More general, and through this long, slow
Erosion we become fit for our safe
Probable worlds and forget there ever was
A distinction to be made between a thing
Wasted or badly used, and one used up.

The Mother's Seduction

for Emily Dickinson

I christen you my mother, and you,
Like her, refuse to give straight answers—
She, silent; you, forever talking slant.

      And I've exhausted all questions except
      The one to which I am answer
      And therefore cannot form.

You deal your words like blades or cards
And to keep the game mysterious
You won't divulge the rules. I never win.
And if I come to you because much time
Has passed since my last meal, you tell a tale
About a crumb that you and Robin feast
Upon, leaving some for charity.

      I know it is not true still I believe.

"There's a pair of us," you say, "don't tell–"
And I will keep your secret much too long
Because the racket of this living shames
Me too. The guiltless are not innocent.
I want to lose this innocence, leave
All guilt behind, learn to live loudly,
Become someone, but you won't tell me how.

      I cannot live as you before me did.
      It is another time, another place,

A different set of circumstances,
A different work to live.

We have no rest to give each other.
The leaves they turn and turn. With tenderness
I touch you out of sleep; I wake to your
Wild words: *much madness is divinest sense.*

We cannot reach each other now though I,
Too, dwell in possibility. Escape
Is on my tongue, still, I can no more run
Away from you than crawl into your arms

●

Miserykids on the Line

●

Shouldn't we have outgrown this desire
Long ago: to be cradled, rocked
Inside the intricate shallows of an ear,
As if our voices held the essential part
Of us, and being heard, the safest way
Of being held, tenuously, unarmed?

Returned as from the dead I find your arms
At last, waiting, nothing left to desire,
And I would to cry the unself-conscious way
A small child cries its hunger to be rocked,
Except within me lies a glaciered part—
Barbed words, debris—that will not let you near.

My mother cut off her first husband's ear
Before she held my dad with other arms—
Their king-size bed, her guns, equally a part
Of what we must call love or strong desire.
Could shots I never heard have really rocked
Me loose from childhood and explain the way

I resist your pull but cannot move away?
An angel, you are terrifying and ir-
Resistible. How effortlessly *rocked*
Wears down to being stoned and healing harms.
Which nonetheless does not erode desire
To be less whole, which is to say, a part.

Faces barely seen and never touched part
Me into many tiny braids; they weigh
On my chest, tense, slacken, derail desire
For ease and grace—you, balanced, in my ear.
Here, as yet, no woman's voice disarms
Me, makes of me an undone thing defrocked

Of all my skins and saving faces, rocked
Open by sure knowledge of departure.
Bodies I sculpt in clay require no arms;
Without hands they are complete, pure the way
A starving girl grows pure—a voice, an ear—
A touch that's free from touch, from need, desire.

Stranded here, rocked shut, I hate the word *desire*,
Hate the way the language holds apart
What strains to close: our arms and voices, ears.

Bitches on the Bright Side

Say what you will, there's something to be said
For desperate calls unanswered, meals alone,
Keeping corners, and lying late in bed.

For bodies over-full but seldom nourished,
For cold and rain that's carried in the bone.
Say what you will, there's something to be said

For useless women raging for more red,
Loud visions urging them to quell the sun
By keeping corners, lying late in bed.

By rising slow and learning from the dead
To feign indifference to light and motion
Let dawn flirt as she will. And something said

For intimate messages baked into bread
Meant for birds that have already flown,
Impatient grown of lying late in bed.

And something more for love that won't be had,
And comfort that's despised until it's gone.
Though bitch we will, the half has not been said
For keeping corners, lying late in bed.

II.

Separation

During the ceremony of sequestration,
the medieval leper knelt at an altar or stood
in an open grave while the priest recited
the ceremony for the burial of the dead.
—Disease of the Soul

The shovel scrapes, slowly the good earth gives.
I close my eyes and open my mouth wide
To taste the dirt cascading over my head,
One shovel-full, then two. *Be dead to the world;*
Be reborn to God. Twice, I struggled to be here, deep
Inside the earth, ached to share a sister's rest.
The women touched me then, their arms at first
Like stone I struggled to break through,
Then giving way to long sweet grass as I,
Exhausted, let myself be lulled by voices,
Bathed by tears, a breast beneath my cheek
As I nursed my own child. Oh God, I mustn't think.
Someone has shoved a ladder down for me.
They'll burn it sure; henceforth I will wear gloves.
The wood is rough, splinters sting my hands.
My eyes tear as I move up into light.
My body is too present, too heavy,
Not light and ghostly as I had imagined.
No magic then inside the priest's slow drone.
The world is neither more beautiful nor more cruel,
Only I have been removed a little distance.
I forbid you to enter the marketplace, mill,
Or fair without your leper's clothes. To touch
Anything you bargain for or buy until
It's yours, to touch a well without your gloves,

29

To walk in narrow lanes. I forbid you
To touch children or give them anything.
I forbid you to touch. The priest's lips
Are pale and thin, the ashen color of berries
Taken by early frost some merchants try to sell.
Holding them lightly on your fingertips,
Stroking with thumb, you can feel the cold curled like
A snake or a child. Some days I've sought such fruit.
There will be those who'll beg to kiss my sores,
But none to take the gifts I'll ache to give.

I bend, take up clapper and clothes, cask and bowl,
My portion of abundance in the world,
And turn toward the appointed place, a hut
On the edge of town, unable to imagine
How I'll say the words required: *This retreat is mine.*
I will live here always because I have chosen it.

●

Separation II

●

His eyes hold only distance. I am dead,
But someone has forgot to tell the sun
Who warms me with his one unblinking eye,
Holds, then burns. Ashes grit my eyes;
Their marble softens, smooths, until the sky
Is streaming—birds, fishes, leaves, or is it
Loaves? In any case the miracle
Is wrong. Desire's what I need. But why
Stand here dreaming. There will be more than time
Enough to dream. Listen, sift the voice
Out from the stones; in memory perhaps
The priest will be a man, his body or,
At least, his secret heart grown tender
Beneath the harshness of his call. *Unchecked*
The impure limb defileth the whole body.
No longer must the wheat grow with the tares.

Burden

after Ben Jonson

Forgive my breath, my loneliness, my eyes;
Absolve me of myself, the many lies
I've told almost daily, and further sin
That flowers on my face and tints my skin.
Forgive me that I've lain in bed all day
Reading poems and nourishing betrayal;
That I can find no thing I love, no friend
To moor me here, a weight against strong wind.
Forgive this rootlessness, my solitude,
The light I've squandered wandering this dark wood.
Harden the hearts of those that I would grieve;
Remove from me this hundred-weight of love.

October Watch

All I've lost is what I have not grieved
—Susan Griffin

Outside the wind is mourning day's lost light.
Inside I wait this dying time alone
Though I would sell my soul to lie with love.

Though I would sell my soul to lie with love,
This reverence for truth that autumn leaves
Keeps me up and honest on my feet
Not well enough for life, too sick to sleep.

Not well enough for life, too sick to sleep,
I slip into a distant time before
Religion was bad poetry and despair
When perfect love of Jesus cast out fear.

When perfect love of Jesus cast out fear,
Faith was strong though living life was hard—
Easy to fall in love with One who bleeds,
Difficult to hold a dying god.

Tonight my hands are empty as I pray
And listen to the letting go of leaves.

Self-Portrait: Indolence and Industry

Morning is coming, but also the night
Seeds sleep in the fields, the golden wheat
Planting promises nothing: harvest, blight

To pray is left, is left while there is light
To spin the voice into the dizzying height
Morning is coming, but also the night

As if it were some thing to trust to flight
A bird, a kite, a boomerang, then wait
Planting promises nothing: harvest, blight

For some return, the ear-drum stretched so tight
The nerve strings snap—stirrup, anvil, hammer, white
Morning is coming, but also the night

As sun-bleached sand. Silence raining drought
Upon the land, the stony heart grows hate
Planting promises nothing: harvest, blight

Like weeds—useless flowers, slight
But persistent as earthworms, mushrooms, heat
Morning is coming, but also the night
Planting promises nothing: harvest, blight

Trust

The day is the Lord's

    To Him we give its hours

The land is the Lord's

    To Him we give its yield

The hands are the Lord's

    To Him we give their labor

The feet are the Lord's

    To Him we give their paths.

The breath is the Lord's

    To Him we give its passing

The eyes are the Lord's

    To Him we give their sight

The mouth is the Lord's

    To Him we give its saying

The bowels are the Lord's

      To Him we give their gripe.

The sky is the Lord's

      We do not breach its distance

The water is the Lord's

      We do not soil its skin

The children are the Lord's

      We lay not our hands upon them

The mountains are the Lord's

      We suffer them to stand.

The rain is the Lord's

      The wheat waits to receive it

The wind is the Lord's

      The trees lift up their arms

The roses are the Lord's

      The world's thorns cannot harm us

When History's wet nurses

      Wrap the world for Him.

A Protocol for Touch

"Keep your colors in the box and hands
To yourself. If the right hand should offend
Cut it off, cast it out; burn
It by moonlight or sow it deep in winter
Ground, and tremble lest the spring should yield
Increase. Say; 'I'm sorry.' should you touch

"Someone without intent, and keep in touch
Exactly when beyond the reach of hands.
Should a stranger cross your path be quick to yield;
The slightest graze of eyes just might offend.
In every season clothe yourself in winter.
Remember: better to marry than to burn."

And those who didn't marry often burned.
Strong tongues of fire like no lover's touch.
How much relief in vivid scenes of winter—
Ice-covered ponds, sleigh rides, and frozen hands?
Only a child, unrecognized as fiend,
No man demanding what she cannot yield.

Year after year he plants but nothing yields;
His palms begin to itch and then to burn.
Abundance mocks him, extravagance offends.
If he could zap her with his Midas touch,
He would expose the trick, the sleight of hand,
Make it his own, and even bear in winter.

In time, she will surrender to his winter,
No longer fight the disappearing, yield
Her body piece by piece starting with hands
Mute and useless inside gloves. No burn
Of sterile priestly fire would ever touch
Her who studied absence not to offend.

"Withhold comfort for this too might offend.
Shroud rude hands in pockets, gloves in winter.
Make lists of those you can and cannot touch.
Guard against unwarranted affection. Yield
To fear alone. To burn within is to burn
Without. Armed with eyes, avoid the risks of hands."

Often she yields her gaze not to offend.
Still, sometimes, inside her winter burns,
And small worlds are clothed in fire by her hands' touch.

Cradle Song: A Found Poem

*An "intelligence test" used to establish "mental
and hereditary illness" in Germany from 1933.
Some 320,000–350,000 people were sterilised in
accordance with these dubious criteria.*
—The Racial State

What is your name?
What are you?
Where is this place?
Who brought you here?

Who are the people around you?

Where does the sun rise?
What does it cost to send a letter?
Why do children go to school?
What does it mean to boil water?

Why does one build houses higher in towns than in the countryside?

Who was Bismarck?
Who was Luther?
What kind of state do we have at present?
What does Christmas mean?

Who discovered America, and when?

What is the difference between:
Mistake and lie? gift and loan?
Saving and parsimony? pond and stream?
Ladder and stairs? having/not having babies?

What is the difference now between night and day?

●

The Bride

●

Her sisters bathe her.
Fold handfuls of lather
Into her pungent oily hair,
And after, pour buckets and buckets
Of steaming spring water
Carried from its source at the mountain's base
Up the long steep trek
Slung over the broad shoulders—
Balancing poles pressed into the back
Of the ruddy necks—of maids,
High-strung as fillies, handsome as mares.
Today the maids have rest.

The sisters done, the mothers come
To anoint the bride with spicery and myrrh,
While in another place, the philosophers
Erect out of the murk and muddle
A path of clear ideas
Leading to the clearing in the forest
Where the nuptials will occur.
The bride will arrive there unsullied
By fallen leaves, her hem untouched by mud.

The poets braid edelweiss,
Lilies, and laurel into her hair,
Singing with the voices of angels while they work.
They linger admiring their own exquisite skill
Until the impatient cooks beat them back,

Anxious to paint the bride's heart-shaped face
With delicately-spiced blends of peaches,
Strawberries, bananas, and cream,
All laced with the subtlest hint, the tiniest taste
Of premium rum. They stuff her mouth
With mint leaves and knead butter and
Almonds and pure vanilla into her breasts and hands.
Her father pronounces her: *No daughter of mine,*
Too absolutely God-damned beautiful!
As he towers over her, his large hands
Clumsy at the intricate lacings of her gloves.
Her brothers declare her: *Good enough to eat;*
Thick spittle snakes down their several chins.
They are only held at bay
By fear of the bridegroom's wrath,
Who after all is waiting. It is time.

But wait. Someone is knocking at the door,
Rushing past the drunken ageing porter.
Who dares to importune them on such a day!
Such insolence will not be tolerated.
Whoever it is must be summarily whipped.
But in the end all weapons are put away,
For it is only the public health inspector
Come upon the bridegroom's business.
The cool eye of science must examine the blushing bride.

He unfastens her white kid boots,
Hook by hook, eye by eye, twists
At her ankles, tugs her ten toes
And checks off the appropriate line
On his sheet. He sits her down on top
Of her father's mahogany wet bar
And hammers at her knees. He checks that off.
He raises her long skirt up over his head
And probes for maggots, probes for fleas,
Sniffs and sniffs to ferret out

Odors suggestive of disease, but she
Is clean. He scrubs her breasts and face
Clean of paints and oils in search of freckles and moles,
An array of imperfections held as marks
Of beauty by a superstitious age, whose day had passed.
Her hair, he parts strand by strand with a mirrored, fine-toothed comb.
No one breathes as the first unlaced glove is peeled back
Revealing the bride's best feature:
Her fine-boned, but strong (capable and strong!) fair hands.

The public health inspector's nostrils flare.
The wart must be removed. Bring him a knife, posthaste.
Or else the whole thing must be called off
And more than likely the entire house will hang
For this, this treason! The family complies,
But where the wart had been is now a scar,
And consequently the finger has to go,
And next the hand, and next the arm, the whole
Side of the body, and the remaining upper half,
And the lower quarter, and what good is the head all by itself?
Just another pretty face. Reduce it all
To ash; the bridegroom will form it new
Inside his hands and breathe into it life.
The bridegroom is patient, willing to wait
Until this, his newborn bride, should attain
Majority. Then they will walk the land together
For one thousand years. Lying down in the dark
Soil, they shall rise with shining children—
Their daughters, perfect mothers, and stalwart
Warriors, their sons. The line of pure-bred night-
Mares shall flourish long.

• • •

I who cannot live among people

I with the German language

This cloud about me.

●

The Faithful Son

●

after Elizabeth Bishop's "The Prodigal"

The cold unyielding silence of the house
Cumbered his movement and racked his breath, so that,
Left to himself, he'd have slept out with the cows,
And left them to their colloquies with ghosts.
At first, he'd hoped with diligence to heal—
Evenings, after the long days' chores, had sat,
Bone-sore on a straight-backed chair, the perfect host,
But they would not be moved; his presence cloyed.
Still, if, after he'd cleared the evening meal
And stoked the fire, he took his hat and coat
Meaning to walk, his mother would avoid
His eyes; the old man accuse him of a whore,
When, in truth, he'd only wanted air.
He'd hesitate a moment, then go out.

Perhaps his love would never come to much
In human terms; he hated scenes. The stars,
The quiet fields, his animals: such
He understood. From where he stood high up
On Shepherd's Hill, he could see for miles—
His brother's tattered form, his father's tears;
He breathed in the revelry and slaughter.
Coarse bread of grief, beetroot, radish, turnip:
Had filled his plate for years; his nerves worn thin.
But now, once more, friends, music, laughter;
Dark rages and darker still betrayals.
That would be his brother's violin.
He looks up at the sky; it looks like rain;
He guesses it is time that he go in.

III.

Avant Garde

I burn to turn a line, tight and funky,
The rhythm of some city in my mouth,
But there is only one time that speaks me:
Molasses days spent lonely in the South.
I got to know this place where I found friends
And learned irreverent love for those long dead.
I took them to my heart or home to bed.
Everything and nothing ever ends.

"You don't sound like you come from Arkansas."
"I thought she was some white girl on the phone,"
An uncle says; this makes my mother proud.
"I think you'd like this book; it's really weird."
". . . You cain't say nothin' nice don't talk at all."
"Eze-kiel connec-ted them dry bones."

Babe

I was unhappy in Louisiana,
Chained to a pack of brats and to a man
Whose joy was only in the saving.
I liked a man with dreams, I had dreams,
But they died soon enough, died with my father.
Look like after that I was mad with the world,
My head was hard; nobody couldn't tell
Me anything. The world seemed hard,
But my heart grew harder. I didn't want
No scholarship from Arkansas Baptist
College or to be a teacher, which had been my dream.
I was second in my class when I quit school.
I was smart and, I guess, real pretty.
The school principal always tried to go with
The brightest girls and that last year, I guess,
It was my turn. I couldn't raise my eyes
'Thout he was there in my line of vision, bearing
Down. That just made me madder until finally
I quit. Not long after I met Cornelius,
And not long after that I married him,
Probably as much out of pure spite as out
Of love. I had the devil in me then.

With him, I moved down to Louisiana.
There was nothing Mama could do to make
Me stay. But as the Scriptures say: Pride goeth
Before a fall. And, believe me, I was proud.
I had a long, long way to fall before

The ground would reach up to slap me, to knock
Some sense into my head the way that Mama
Had as long as she thought it'd do
Some good, before rage swept me far beyond
The reach of her two hands. After Daddy
Died, there was just us, two women, which
Didn't amount to much of anything
In my book then. Woman plus a woman
Would never make a home. Mark how even
In the Book of Ruth the story turns on men—
Husbands and sons. I was married twelve long years
Before my womb would bear. That emptiness
Slowly ate away my pride and left me
Humble, wanting nothing beyond a little
Life. When I finally accepted everything—
Cornelius' baby girl that wasn't
Mine, my barren womb, the right of life
To leave or stay away—I bore a son,
So big and beautiful! The comfort of
My age. Five more babies came after him,
But he was special, the only one I named
Pleasing no one but myself. When he became
A man he threw half that name away;
Cleophas wasn't good enough for him,
But he is mine. He visits often, phones
Me everyday. I can depend on him
For anything I need. Mostly I call
Him Brother or sometimes Knucklehead.
Both his daughters carry pieces of
My name: Wanda Lee and Constance Rose.
Rosie Lee's my name, Walker before
I married.

   Brother was eight or nine when I
Finally had enough of trying to starve
Out life to feed a dream: next year
A bigger crop, saving so he could buy

This or that piece of land. A piece of ribbon,
The cloth for a new apron or a dress,
A book or little trinket, more visits home—
He said *no* to all, or *yes, but later* . . .
After . . . Always after this thing or that.
Each time he would say *when*, I could hear him
Saying *never*. I wrote home to Mama.
She came as soon as she could find someone
To drive her. I never will forget how she
Came strolling in, piss proud like a man.
She had a pistol and a bottle
Of gin which she laid out on the table
Like playing cards. *Cornelius, I've come at Babe.*
That's what she said, *Cornelius, I've come at Babe.*
Man to man, just like that. I had
Packed already. We left next morning after
Breakfast. Me and Mama and the kids.
Cornelius packed up all his farming tools
And joined us in Arkansas a little later.
But from that day forward me and Mama lived
In houses that stood side by side—during
The time we stayed in Shilo and after
We moved to town, right up until the day
She died.

　　Seven years ago, Cornelius died.
I've buried one of our three daughters, her
Youngest daughter, and one of her grandsons.
Someone braids my hair straight down my back,
Coiling it tight and fixing it fast with pins—
Not like Mama's hands but doing as
They once did for me, as mine for her.
It is her beard that I shave now from
My face, that pushes out in little wisps
Under my grand-daughter's smooth chin. Brother's
Baby girl. The one who makes me tell
So many stories and is never satisfied,

And remembers everything. She hasn't told
Me yet, but when I'm dead she'll have this stick
I use to walk now and again since
I fell and broke my hip. Of everything
I have that's what she wants. It was Mama's
Before it came to me, and came to her
Also from someone else. Brother will need
It before too long, before it's done
With me if he don't slow down, admit
That he's grown old and retire like someone
With good sense. After him, the walking stick
Is hers, a little something to go with
The beard and name and, possibly, the fire.
What I want is for someone to call me, *Babe*.

The Ghost Child

Like a guilty one in secret I return
To the time, the space where violence first unfurled
Its sleek and silent wings amid green life—
The parking lot outside Mad Butcher's store.
I reenact the scene of justice served
Or callous crime, as it was overheard
So long ago. I piece the scraps of talk
That I remember together with frail threads
That I invent, frantic to give a form
To what's denied, give reasons for the way
My faith is spent. I could have been an orphan—
Father dead and mother fled aboard
Some Greyhound bus to parts unknown—
But Dad was fine except one kidney lost,
And Mom made bail and later, charges dropped,
And everyone survived no worse for wear;
Broke bread, fought fights, lived on, forgave, forgot.

Debriefing

After I got shot
I died on the table,
Heard them say: he's gone.
But I came back. Scared?
Naw, I wasn't scared,
But I came back. Just
Came on back.

Come here, let me show you.
'Case somethin' happen
To me. Just a little somethin'
I've saved. Right here, under
This here rug; it'll be right here.
Are you list'nin' to me? Now don't
You go tellin' Sister and Dad 'cause
They don't need to know. And oh,
See here, I got a whole sock tied
Up full of change; it'll be
Way back here, behind of this here
Drawer . . . Why I'm tellin' you?
'Cause I know I can trus' my baby,
And you'll remember when time comes.

I'm sick and tired of playing your stupid baby games!

At least I'm not afraid to sleep alone, mama's baby!

•

I was just sayin' to Brother
I don't know what make you young folks
Want to take yourselves so far
Off to live, where your poor old
Gran'ma cain't even get a look at ya
Now and again. You must be studyin' on
Findin' you some britches. Pretty soon
You'll be back down here bringin' some britches with ya.

•

No, Ma'amma, it's studying
I'm studyin' on. Nothing to do
With britches. Believe me, nothing at all.

Listen to me. Listen
To the silence. What
I tell you is never
What I tell you
But something else.

Etude for Memory and Guitar

I. Two Sisters

> *Is patient's ocular condition believed to have*
> *occurred in any blood relative(s)?*
>
> *Yes, father and sister.*
>
> —*Physician's Report of Eye Examination*

It is not unlikely that you will find the sisters quite alike. You will be amused by their likeness and find them, all around, quite likable girls. Indeed, you will be amazed by how little there is to dislike.

While remarking how they look alike—squinting through clouded eyes that flit and dart like small, frightened birds—it is just like you not to notice the tallness of one, the beauty of the other, or how one is quite quiet and the other otherwise.

As for the sisters, they see little or no resemblance and care, not a jot, for all such musings.

II. Ward

I can't remember the weight or lightness of your hands as you fastened buttons, tied sashes. Only the way my body shrank from this, the only touch you gave, afraid of falling into it.

Other things remain palpable: the night cries of the girl who had seizures, the sound of you rubbing her arm, and the ill-will I wished the white girls each morning, as I, in day-old braids, stood off to one side and watched you comb their hair.

III. An Old Story

Little Rock, 1978

Growing up, I had a double. We were the same age and even shared birthdays, not to mention big-boned bodies and less-than-perfect eyes.

Stuck, for years, as reluctant shower buddies because of the sameness of our race, we made the best of it and chose for our bosom friends two petite white girls, who doubled as daughters and slaves.

We had the care of their bodies—combed their hair and chose their clothes each day. We kept them warm in our narrow beds and beat them in the bathroom after hours.

IV. At Nine

From the window in the practice room door, anyone with sight can see them—the girl awkwardly positioned between the bench and the piano, and the older boy above her, prick and hands in her pants.

Which does not absolve the blind bandmaster, who, had he a mind to, would hear how no one in this room ever plays the clarinet, and how the girl, hitherto adequate, is not progressing.

V. Revision

People are trying to kill me. At home, I fear my sister most; at school, the kitchen workers.

Of course, I don't fear all the kitchen workers. Only the women.

Only the women who are black.

VI. Power Play

My best friend, Tamara, had one glass eye. She used to take it out upon command so that our keeper would have to let us out to see the nurse who'd pop the eye back in.

We especially liked to pull this stunt at night—the silence of our supposed sleep disturbed by Tammy crying that her eye fell out. (She did hysteria well.)

And even if the matron did suspect something amiss, her hands were tied. For what else can you do, confronted with a beautiful, sniveling child, one blind eye in her head and one in hand, except to send her out into the night—far from your perfect vision—accompanied by a train of closest friends?

As a Child

She says she stuttered,
But the others who don't
Remember say she doesn't
Didn't, she means, back then
Not now, back then, those years
When there were oxen on
Her tongue. She says, guesses,
She is wrong, stuttered only
Maybe at school, maybe never
At home. Her father thinks
He almost remembers, finally
Doesn't, or at least cannot be sure,
So she thinks maybe she didn't
But does now or might in future,
Remains aware of the risk
If she's not careful, not fast
Enough or hesitates too long
Not long enough, she means.
If she's not careful, not fast
Enough or hesitates too . . . not too . . .
Long enough [she listens] *What? What*
Will Happen? They'll think she's telling
Stories—not *very* or *frighteningly*
Convincing ones like when she is
A murdering Nazi or German
Jew on Holocaust exams—
But stories that wear their insides
Out like a father's colostomy

Bag, changed by an angry older
Sister. Where was Mom? And *was* she
Angry? Was she [the sister] ten? Nine?
And the stutterer, the story-
Teller, counter of costs,
Teller of lie lives?

•

What Then? A Riddle

•

Having grown, but never (not quite)
Safely out of the besieged body
Of a child into full armor fused
With skin—let us call it "life" . . .

IV.

Self-Portrait: Lilith, Eve

The austere angels dozing at their posts,
The flaming sword floats between us like
A bridal veil stirred by breath or wind,
Utterly transparent and vulnerable
To tears at slightest touch. So how explain
This chronic failure of eyes, of hands, to meet?
Those who come after will say it was
He who hulked between us like a wall
Of rock dividing countries, estranging
Sea from land. Will say that I abandoned
You to a life I would not stand. Or, I
Supplanted you in the garden with the man.

Not in the slightest do we grudge them
The comfort of such myths, neither can we
Forget what we have known:
An orange presence in a circle of stones.
How it seemed to leap inside us as we stroked
The length of his unfurled body over
And over with our tongue. How live things seemed
To clench and ripple just beneath his skin.
How his body was a flask full of brightness
Spilt with little provocation.
How easily stopped his breath; how fragile his bone.
How we could not tell his heartbeat from our own.

Some mornings the ground was strewn with flowers torn
From their stalks by wind; the world was quiet then.

No, too ablaze with sound. What happened then?
Nothing. And after that? Nothing. There is
No story here. Bending above his body,
Tending its delicate milkweed flower,
We trembled with pleasure to hold such power
Over him. For me there was no pleasure,
And I was still and very much afraid.
Little by little you began to leave
The garden? Yes, as more and more you stayed.
Nothing clean or simple about that split.

And it's still ongoing. Too soon to sort it out.
One good eye, one breast, two hands, a single tongue
Between us—how we wrestle over words,
Strain to wring some blessing from the silence,
Deliverance from violence, its fear, its lure,
The tyranny of names: night day,
Sable and alabaster, flint shale,
Steel and lace. Who among us can afford
To speak the language—any language—rightly?
As if it weren't enough to bear one heart
Eternally divided in its chambers.

We stand close enough to touch. We do
Not touch. Between us burns a sword of fire,
A rusted turnstile glinting in the sun.

●

Exile

●

The air is dry in this much-promised land,
And mountains whisper "this is not your home";
Still nights entice me like a knowing hand,
And strangers' hands have sometimes brushed my own.
Yet milk, so sweet, turns rancid in my mouth,
And I can name no answer to desire
Since God is everywhere and I'm without.
I taste the stone's sleek kiss, lie with each hour
And dream of taking up my staff and rod,
Of no longer lingering weary at the door
My hands heavy with holy tears for God
Or some woman who always fails to come.
But it's hard to leave the vigil once begun,
And waiting soon becomes much more than for.

•

Embrace

•

Leaves pressed against the pane stare
While the tiny, unobtrusive tear
In the fabric where the poems are

Suffers some new stress and grows
Beautiful and bloody as a rose,
While Art refuses what it owes

The heart, the chafing wind, the body's strain
To hold at once the distant train,
Its own soft breath, tattoo of rain

That worries the world's rough skin until it glistens.
The ear speaks, the mouth listens.
In shadowy boutiques under the sea, the poet redeems bright suns

For wishes, or kisses maybe, depending on availability.
Leaves like girls murmur [protective of their prodigious ability
For song] snatches of not-quite-melody under their breath, ever so lightly.

Tonight the world's racket—leaves, heart, wind, rain—swarms
Inside the body's shell—no peaceful, distant, soothing song, but cold
    waves crashing down; the light we give rarely warms
Us, or warms but not enough. And it is almost worse than being unheld,
    to lie cradled in the circle of our own frail arms.

Pantoum: Morning

You eat or not; you bathe or not;
Brush hair or teeth or dress or not;
Then sit at your desk to read or write.
You do not ask to be or not.

Brush hair or teeth or dress or not,
You know your place; you make your stand;
No longer ask if it's to be or not
This struggle with the page and pen.

You know your place; you try to stand
Up on the slippery backs of words.
You struggle over page and pen.
No *peace, be still!* quite calms your rage.

Up on the slippery backs of words,
You hope they'll swallow you like whales.
How peaceful, still inside that rage,
A dark as dark as lighted page.

You hope they'll swallow you quite whole,
A belly like your mother's womb,
A dark as dark as lighted page,
A room as soft as sea or loam.

A belly like your mother's womb?
Something once read or learned by rote;
A room as soft as sea or loam?
A questioned poised: *to be or not?*

Who Claims the Poets?

Not me. Anyway, not here, not now, and
Certainly not like this. I wait, but end
Usually by turning away nothing said.
And it's not that I am shy or even
Impatient; only what is there to say?
Listening to you read that poem I forgot
To breathe? Did not remember until you asked
If we were all okay? And then, there's space.
I rise early, dress, and trudge through snow,
Burning to ask one question about one poem,
But the poet's late and when she comes, there are
These introductions as if our names could matter.
And then, questions that crowd close into her answers,
Offending my puritan sense of order:
Each voice contained within its clear white border.

But that's not right. It's how I'd never touch
A stranger, rarely a friend, or nudge my way
Into a conversation; often retreat from those
In which, I think, I'm welcomed, always not
Quite sure. It's a coarse and naked thing, the voice;
And silence a swaddling blanket, heavy
As deep sleep or water. The surface comes
But slowly. Before the sentence of the air
There's belly, chest, and throat; alphabet
And dictionary. So I wait for the wave
To build, for the wide wake to recede,
But these others walk on water, ride the waves,

Set their voices down like helicopters,
Insinuate their bodies where there's no room,
Leaving me suspecting Woolf, indeed, was right:
One ought to sink to the bottom of the sea,
Probably, and live alone with ones words.
Or, less dramatically, to be a stone
Worried by water as your words, late
at night in empty rooms, worry my voice
Until it's raw and no longer mine.

●

Tell

●

How she remembers spring,
The force of body's hunger
For all things good to eat:

Broccoli spears and cauliflower
With slightly-seasoned sour
Cream, strawberries plain.

How she adored pasta,
Found praise for soup and salad,
Ate her bread unbroken;

The apple and the olive
A symbol for no thing.

Eschewed the soft sweet token
Of chimeric satisfaction:
Chocolate aping love;

Lured instead by eggs and grapes,
Peas laced with onion pearls,
The prune's dark juice, and cheese

Of any kind. How she thought,
Feared she must be dying,
Wholly unrecognizing
The deep root as her own.

How indiscriminating
It was, how rude! Its taste
Singularly bad and out of place
In lighted dining rooms.

How she was just alive.

II
How summer still unsettled
Would find her body lulled,
Replete with its well-being
Like sun-light flooded rooms.

Exiled from further wanting,
Untouched by healing's good,
How food became a bother,
A duty necessary,
Exterior to her will and her desire.

How it swallowed up her time,
Destroyed the day's smooth face
Until it seemed to her
A field picked clean by crows.

How no rebellion rose,
No choice was ever made,
Only a lack of time,
A deep forgetting brought

Back again to mind
By gut's sharp gnaw, new rhythms
In the heart, the moon unhung.

How she watched the page with wonder.
How her hands were sure and gentle.
How the wild bird still would tremble.

How winter never was.

●

Undersong

●

How much to buy a suicide?
What discount if I tried but failed?

Like trousers dropped, the unveiled face
Discloses grace too frail, uncouth

For eyes. Yet, still truth's hum, its marathon
Along these tangled avenues?

Stop the blues, the beat of reds and greens?
No subtle charm, nor Christ new come,

Not even Emily's curious wine
Will give again this hurt, this modest hymn:

Cold warms itself inside the body's fire;
The bed-clothes bless with heat until I rise—

The spending of this meager loaf of air
And salt and sun. Light that won't be wooed,

Dedicate to her own pleasure; milk that flows
Regardless of who loves or sleeps

Alone; some final trace of sweetness
Passed from fingertip to tongue. Solace

And shock of almost any touch; voices.
The heart's insistent undersong: *how live?*

How live? how live?

Lullaby

Say to me: out there are only streets, and cars
Are only cars, and childhood lessons of
Both ways will never fail you now. I'd listen
Even if you whispered, strain my ears to hear
The way I silence other voices.
Random ones. I told you of the child.
How when she slept in her crib I could hear
Her crying everywhere—in noises the
House made, in heat and running water, even
Inside the breath of early morning,
My breath, the crying of this child not even
Mine, and she so peacefully asleep.

I can shut my lids on angels, bite my tongue,
Withhold my breath, swallow unbidden words
Before they form. But how to stop my ears?
I can't resist the charm that distance holds:
The silence of a street minutes before
I cross into the constant flow of traffic,
Or sobs that I hear buried in the laughter
Of a girl that make me wait above my book
In terror. As if she had no friends, had need
Of my concern. What is this love I'd heap
Upon the world like blankets unasked for?
And by what right do I stand eavesdropping here?

Ghazal

Listen, in the distance the sound of calling voices:
Hysteric wind shouting down leaves' loud brawling voices.

Innocence lies complicit as paper, while breathing
Comes hard to everything in winter, stalling voices.

The student wakes in a garden strewn with odd flowers;
They lie like stones under his head, not wholly voiceless.

That summer a hole grew in her soul; consult her socks
For proof. Echoes haunt the pavement recalling voices.

A mystery: why we never tasted magnolias?
Why they alone remained unkissed and falling, voiceless?

Feeling God's eye upon her like strong lye licking skin,
She took the tongues inside and sang them dull and voiceless.

She learned her colors from the deluxe Crayola box;
The colors cried out their names with mad, roiling voices.

Lilac lay like lack on the land, littering the lake;
Faith, bright fish, leaps in all the water's flowing voice says.

The proximate alone merits constant attention;
The dumb heart learns to follow where the darling voice is.

A Riddle: Old Saws, Eloquent Squawkings

> *Words / Are what friends, not lovers, have*
> *between them, / Old saws, eloquent squawkings.*
> —*J. D. McClatchy, "An Essay on Friendship"*

Something precious. Something
Hard and brittle. Broken
How many times? Held
By children's glue and string.
Something priceless. Someone
Not yet, not quite, you.

For you, business as usual—
Something borrowed, something
Blue: someone missing someone
Vaguely, the record unbroken
But scratched, stuck on a string
Of vowels, sharp breath inhaled

And holding, holding, held.
It would be cruel to touch you,
Taut as the high E string
Just before it gave and something
Snapped. No talent for the broken,
The guitar I left with someone

Is quiet, or maybe someone
Lifts it from where it's held
To smooth the brow of broken
Sleep, a lullaby for you,
The feverish world, something
Rapt by absence and string.

From the rush of babble heft and string
Words dripping with someone
Else's silence, something
Said over until it held
Itself apart, a note that you
Can't hear or reach. Broken

Record: *May the circle be unbroken.*
Around your neck a string
Of perfect pearls. Confusing you
Always always with someone
I should or might have held
Or shouldn't have. Something

Broken, broken, caught and held.
Something language, a filament between you.
Someone patiently restringing the guitar.

•

Genesis

•

In the beginning was the Word, and the
Word was with God and the Word was God.
The same was in the beginning with God.
All things were made by him; and without
him was not anything made that was made.
—*John 1:1–3*

Even when her dial is firmly turned to off
Cold sweet milk is the one thing she can't quite
Get enough of. That, and words that rival
God for taste. For Eucharist, she would
Say plain "eating God," an index of
Her passion and her hunger. Sated,
The sacred flesh and blood, like too much
Of any food, soon sickened. . . . Or
Was it how the Psalter fell
From the mouth of the congregation
Like styrofoam, clumsy, useless, irrevocably man-made?
Nothing like the one other-worldly voice
Of her New Hartford nuns breaking into
Two, again to come together just
Before the accretion of caesuras rained
Too beautiful to bear. How they could yawn
And never miss a beat. A house of women
Bound by a book of common prayer, their words
As real as flesh as real as any Word.
Each day, a sweet orange slowly peeled
The while we slept protected by magic
Overskins woven by our voices at compline.
The fruit fed to us in succulent sections,
The better to be shared and to be savored,

Flavored everything: the light, the rain, the fall
Of Great Silence, talk of money ending in harsh words.
We sucked that juice until only pulp remained,
Then seeds, slippery as words we learn
To live by—*loss, faith*—too big to get
Our arms around, too small to tear with teeth.
The perpetual impossibility
Of leaving, staying anywhere. The lure
And lie of motion, the terror of relief.

A storm raging outside, my back turned to
The cross, I sat on the edge of my bed reading
Rilke's *Duino Elegies.* Without
Sobs from the lining of the gut that seem
Almost to burst the throat, I wept for all
I'd lost. Rather, for what I'd found the second
Time, and yet still could not hold. And in the sun,
Before the flowers' faces and well in view of God
Or any one, again the stream of tears
As I sat trying to read the magazine
Loaned me by Sister Cornelia.
Lazarus, you were the friend Jesus could
Not live without, so when you died of not
Being sure of that, he wept until your name
Rolled out of him like thunder: please, I need
You; please, come out! I hold the tiny seeds
Inside my hands, warm them with my breath,
Sow them in the richest soil I know,
Yet only silence blooms astonishing
As absence. *Someone within these walls has been*
In love with Death longer than I care to say;
It was not you! . . . but he gets in that way.
O, Helen, Katie, Lisa, Laura,
Tamara, Michelle, . . . I pull the open book
Close to my breast, caress its back, its spine.
Not recognizing this as another woman's
Gesture, I rest my head on her shoulder,

Gently kiss the forehead so well-lined.
Surely the places you are fail to
Rival this light I'm bathed in now, the feel
Of covers against my cheek, under my hands,
Sweet milk so amply flowing from these dark veins,
Like God, like honey, like blood, like love, like milk,
Into and from the desert of this mouth.

The Check-Out Lady at the IGA

No angels, no anger, no death, no despair,
No room for all that in a poem about Sarah—
Sarah in blue shorts, pink tank distracting,
Sarah of the unspectacular hair (neither
Red nor flaming fuchsia), voice I'd know anywhere.

And someone will ask, why write a poem for Sarah?—
Sarah whom you do not love or even know well,
Sarah untouched by death who cannot haunt you,
Unimagined by want and incapable
Of raining insanity or peace into your mind?

Someone will ask, but I will not answer.
Why write poems for the dead who will not forsake
Their graves and send no invitations?
Or for those sexy-boned ones who will not stay
Or leave your life guillotine clean?

A poem about Sarah, a poem about
The check-out lady at the IGA,
About any damned thing or blessed body
Is not impossible or against the laws
(Assuming I had any respect for the laws).

So go ahead, cry wolf, betrayal, outrage.
Your dismal daughter has turned from your ways.
This is no sad-assed melancholy poem
About civilization and its discontents.
This is a poem about Sarah.

● Offering ●

The climate changes, the place names change, but still
There are these women who offer pasta
And tell the truth—as if God, called suddenly
Away, sent angels in his place to await
My coming. Under orders, they give nothing
Beyond what is sufficient for strength
And hunger. Meanwhile, or so I imagine,
Of me they ask everything, exacting
Much more than I am aware of having.
They offer no rest, in fact, refuse it,
And in their arms and voices carry fleeting
Traces of what I now imagine home
Might be. They bless then banish me to search.

Failures are what I remember. They alone
Provide occasions for crude monuments
To mark the path that will lead us back to the place
Where I held out my hand and you—seeing
In me only what I lacked, wealth, beauty,
Poise, and perfect eyes—misread the sign
And turned away thinking it was for you
To give or not to give. Understand this:
We do not get what we deserve. There is
No reason that I should have no child, should not
Be dead or jaded, or too tired at day's end
Or lacking in desire to sit late
Making poems. There is no reason why
This body—ears, hands, belly, mouth,

An aggregate of bowls—should be filled
To overflowing while others go without.
Out of greed or courtesy I take what's given,
Then move away reeling from the weight, hands
Outstretched for balance, and in invitation:
I know that you are whole. But so much so
That you have nothing further to receive?

•

Ars Poetica

•

Language belongs to the other, someone says,
It doesn't matter who; I haven't read him.
The axiom is true nevertheless;
I've seen the proof spun out in daily practice:
For instance, people tend to riddle me
With questions, to draw me out, I guess, but it
Soon becomes an Echo-and-Narcissus
Situation in which I can say nothing of
My own, but only give the other back her speech.
So how am I supposed to talk to you,
Waiting there as silent as the lake
That gives the sky the sky, the boy the boy?
Only a fool doesn't understand
He loved the river, too. I'd say the world
Is flush with fools. But did Narcissus know
He loved the lake? It's like that Margaret Atwood poem
I read you, "Tricks with Mirrors": a mirror
Or a lake's work mostly goes unnoticed.
In the beholder's eye the clear unwavering
Reflection just happens in the normal course
Of things, requiring no art, no skill,
No labor. And wouldn't they admit it—mirrors,
Lakes—that as games go, it's a damned good game
As long as you're playing for low stakes.
When stakes are high the position quickly turns
Precarious: say, you answer truly to
The queen—she's getting on, no longer fair,
Has many younger rivals in the kingdom—

Or, say, Narcissus sees cruelty's
Deep shadow hardening his face, dimming
His eyes. They'll think the fault's in you. He'll throw
Stone after stone until his visage comes
Back clear; she'll stamp her foot and ask and ask
Again day after day, year after year
Or smash you with a hairbrush or a shoe,
Pick up the phone and order a new mirror.
Mirrors are never irreplaceable
Though often they will tell you otherwise.
At last, exhausted, he will fling himself
At you, and you will hide him deep within
Your heart—in time, you will become a vast
Graveyard, lost shoes, old loves, black fears,
A long century's bitter, unwept tears . . .

On the face of it, you haven't lost a thing.
Your patience you still have, your art, your power
Of attention, your rage for self-effacement,
And after all, there will be other faces.
Only . . . only a fool could fail to see
That the lake loved Narcissus as Echo did,
Loved the difference, would have stayed separate.
Why, why under heaven, should the twain be one—
Real or imaginary, loving or beloved?
But who among us stoops to comprehend
The passion of a lake, stops to imagine?
See how she recognizes everything,
Excludes nothing, quietly exercises
(No hoopla here!) diversity and justice.
See how she tempers truth with tenderness,
Makes a mottled quilt of separateness,
A flowing out of stillness. She means no harm.
Attention is the purest face of love.
So why then is it suspect and so rare?
She only saw her face, not my face there.

And when I speak in answer to their questions,
Spoken and unspoken, or move within
The scripted expectations, it's not my voice they hear.
Find your own voice, the writing hucksters say,
Write what you know. And go on knowing only what
We know? And never know the lakeness of the lake?